MW00900331

MY

GRATITUDE

JOURNAL

MIRABELL PUBLISHING

Dear Parents,

Gratitude is a learned attitude. We live in
a world that gets more materialistic and
selfish every day and it is important to
teach children from a very early age the art
of being thankful.

Keeping a gratitude journal will help your
child develop sensitivity and appreciate
the world.

Happy Journaling!

Mirabell Publishing

I AM

GRATEFUL

FOR

HOW TO USE YOUR GRATITUDE JOURNAL

Each day your child will write down three things for which he or she is grateful for. This might be:

- Something that happened to them that day
- Something a friend did for them
- Something they have
- Something they did for someone else

Let your child explain why he or she is thankful for this item and then draw a picture or stick a photograph to illustrate it.

At the end of each week read over the entries together and talk about them.

DATE

I'M GRATEFUL FOR...

I'M GRATEFUL FOR...

I'M GRATEFUL FOR...

Don't forget to put today's date

List three things that made today great!

Paste your pictures or draw what you are grateful for today!

I am grateful for such good friends and family today love

Paste a Picture or Draw what you are grateful for today!

Gratitude Journals are a great way to teach kids to appreciate what they have. Keeping a gratitude journal helps kids develop better attitudes, sensitivity and building closer relationships with family, friends and the world around them.

I'M GRATEFUL FOR...

I'm grateful for my family

I'M GRATEFUL FOR...

I'M GRATEFUL FOR...

Paste your pictures or draw what you are grateful for today!

I'M GRATEFUL FOR...

My School

I'M GRATEFUL FOR...

My house

I'M GRATEFUL FOR...

My friends

Paste your pictures or draw what you are grateful for today!

I'M GRATEFUL FOR...

I'M GRATEFUL FOR...

I'M GRATEFUL FOR...

Paste your pictures or draw what you are grateful for today!

DATE

I'M GRATEFUL FOR...

I'M GRATEFUL FOR...

I'M GRATEFUL FOR...

Paste your pictures or draw what you are grateful for today!

I'M GRATEFUL FOR...

I'M GRATEFUL FOR...

I'M GRATEFUL FOR...

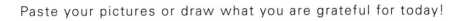

Paste your pictures or draw what you are grateful for today!

I'M GRATEFUL FOR...

I'M GRATEFUL FOR...

I'M GRATEFUL FOR...

Paste your pictures or draw what you are grateful for today!

I'M GRATEFUL FOR...

I'M GRATEFUL FOR...

I'M GRATEFUL FOR...

Paste your pictures or draw what you are grateful for today!

DATE

I'M GRATEFUL FOR...

I'M GRATEFUL FOR...

I'M GRATEFUL FOR...

20

Paste your pictures or draw what you are grateful for today!

I'M GRATEFUL FOR...

I'M GRATEFUL FOR...

I'M GRATEFUL FOR...

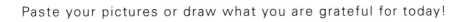

Paste your pictures or draw what you are grateful for today!

I'M GRATEFUL FOR...

I'M GRATEFUL FOR...

I'M GRATEFUL FOR...

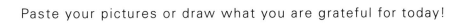

Paste your pictures or draw what you are grateful for today!

I'M GRATEFUL FOR...

I'M GRATEFUL FOR...

I'M GRATEFUL FOR...

Paste your pictures or draw what you are grateful for today!

DATE

I'M GRATEFUL FOR...

I'M GRATEFUL FOR...

I'M GRATEFUL FOR...

Paste your pictures or draw what you are grateful for today!

I'M GRATEFUL FOR...

I'M GRATEFUL FOR...

I'M GRATEFUL FOR...

Paste your pictures or draw what you are grateful for today!

I'M GRATEFUL FOR...

I'M GRATEFUL FOR...

I'M GRATEFUL FOR...

Paste your pictures or draw what you are grateful for today!

I'M GRATEFUL FOR...

I'M GRATEFUL FOR...

I'M GRATEFUL FOR...

Paste your pictures or draw what you are grateful for today!

I'M GRATEFUL FOR...

I'M GRATEFUL FOR...

I'M GRATEFUL FOR...

Paste your pictures or draw what you are grateful for today!

DATE

I'M GRATEFUL FOR...

I'M GRATEFUL FOR...

I'M GRATEFUL FOR...

38

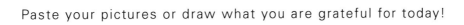

Paste your pictures or draw what you are grateful for today!

I'M GRATEFUL FOR...

I'M GRATEFUL FOR...

I'M GRATEFUL FOR...

Paste your pictures or draw what you are grateful for today!

I'M GRATEFUL FOR...

I'M GRATEFUL FOR...

I'M GRATEFUL FOR...

Paste your pictures or draw what you are grateful for today!

I'M GRATEFUL FOR...

I'M GRATEFUL FOR...

I'M GRATEFUL FOR...

Paste your pictures or draw what you are grateful for today!

I'M GRATEFUL FOR...

I'M GRATEFUL FOR...

I'M GRATEFUL FOR...

Paste your pictures or draw what you are grateful for today!

I'M GRATEFUL FOR...

I'M GRATEFUL FOR...

I'M GRATEFUL FOR...

Paste your pictures or draw what you are grateful for today!

I'M GRATEFUL FOR...

I'M GRATEFUL FOR...

I'M GRATEFUL FOR...

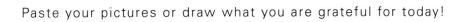

Paste your pictures or draw what you are grateful for today!

I'M GRATEFUL FOR...

I'M GRATEFUL FOR...

I'M GRATEFUL FOR...

Paste your pictures or draw what you are grateful for today!

I'M GRATEFUL FOR...

I'M GRATEFUL FOR...

I'M GRATEFUL FOR...

Paste your pictures or draw what you are grateful for today!

OTHER JOURNALS FROM MIRABELL PUBLISHING

We have the following other journals you may be interested in, which are all available on Amazon:

GRATITUDE JOURNALS

- Gratitude Journal for Kids: My Gratitude Journal
- Gratitude Journal for Kids: 30 Days of Gratitude
- Gratitude Journal for Kids: 52 Weeks of Gratitude
- Gratitude Journal for Kids: 365 Days of Gratitude

TRAVEL JOURNALS

5 - 9 years
- My Travel Journal: A Journal for 5 Family Vacations
- My Travel Journal: A Journal for 10 Family Vacations

10 - 15 years
- My Travel Journal: A Journal for 5 Family Vacations
- My Travel Journal: A Journal for 10 Family Vacations

For flowers that bloom about our feet;

For tender grass, so fresh, so sweet;

For song of bird, and hum of bee;

For all things fair we hear or see,

Father in heaven, we thank Thee!

- Ralph Waldo Emerson

CPSIA information can be obtained at www.ICGtesting.com
Printed in the USA
LVIW01n1923251215
467855LV00001B/1